The Gluten-Free Vegetarian Cookbook

Ann Brooke-Webb

contents

soup

QUICK TOMATO SOUP	9
PUMPKIN & ORANGE SOUP	11
BROCCOLI & STILTON SOUP	13
CARROT & ONION SOUP	15
FRENCH ONION SOUP	17
CRACKERBREAD	19

salads

GREEK SALAD	23
SALATE TRICOLORE	25
STRAWBERRY & PARMESAN SALAD	27
LEMON & SAFFRON COUSCOUS	29
BEETROOT & GOAT CHEESE SALAD	31
WATERMELON & FETA	33
WALDORF SALAD	35

main courses

HOMEMADE PASTA	39
SPINACH RISOTTO	41
GREEK OMELETTE	43
CHEDDAR QUICHE	45
VODKA PENNE	47
FENNEL GRATIN	49

contents

main courses

CASHEW NUT CURRY	51
ALMOND BALLS	53
ITALIAN ALMOND BALLS	55
KORMA ALMOND BALLS	57
SPICY ALMOND BALLS	59
MANICOTTO	61
GLUTEN-FREE PIZZA	63
PASTA CAPRESE	65
BUBBLE & SQUEAK	67
LEMON SPAGETTI	69
POLPETTONE	71
GREEK VEGGIE MOUSSAKA	73
INDIAN LENTIL DHAL	75
MACARONI & CHEESE	77
BUTTERNUT SQUASH CURRY	79
COURGETTE PASTA	81

desserts

CHOCOLATE ICE CREAM	85
ETON MESS	87
SPANISH LEMON CAKE	89
STICKY CHOCOLATE CAKE	91
MERINGUE SWISH	93
APPLE CRUMBLE	95
GLUTEN-FREE WAFFLES	97
BLUEBERRY CHEESECAKE	99

intro...

The news that you have to hold a strict gluten-free diet for the rest of your life might feel a bit daunting at first. But don't despair. Gluten intolerance forces you to start reading the ingredients on food and after the initial shock of what your favourite food contains- a new healthy life can begin. Just because you have to follow a certain diet there is no reason not to treat yourself to the best food you can get hold of. There is also no reason to spend all your spare time in the kitchen (unless, of course, you want to). Many of the recipes in this book are quick to make, some only take 10 minutes. With quick and tasty recipes at hand it is never boring to cook your own food. Eating home cooked food is so much tastier and your body will thank you for all the extra nutrition it gains. The recipes in this book have been collected by me over the years and made into gluten-free and vegetarian meals. I hope you will enjoy the recipes as much as I do.

Ann Brooke-Webb

suggestions...

Stock I use a gluten-free vegetarian stock cube in the recipes where stock is needed. It is a good idea to look at the ingredient list of products often. I know of a few incidences where the company has suddenly changed recipes, so you can never be 100% sure its gluten-free unless you check regularly.

Gluten-Free Flour The only way to find a good gluten-free flour that works for you is to test and try. Some people exclusively use potato, corn or rice flour. I prefer a ready mixture of all three.

Baking powder and other ingredients Always, always read the content list before you use anything. Gluten can appear in the things you would least expect for example baking powder and cocoa powder. Different countries have different brands of food, so it is impossible to suggest any brands. The only way is to always read contents and then test and try.

Thickening of sauces There are many different gluten-free products to use when thickening sauces. A little bit of cold water and a teaspoon of potato flour or corn flour works well too. Just add directly to sauce and stir. Add a little bit at the time until you receive the desired consistency of the sauce.

Pasta In this book you find a recipe for homemade gluten-free pasta. You might want to use ready made pasta, because it is quick and easy. There is an abundance of different makes of gluten-free pasta on the market. Taste is personal and the only way to find your favourites is to test and try.

soups

QUICK TOMATO SOUP
PUMPKIN & ORANGE SOUP
BROCCOLI & STILTON SOUP
CARROT & ONION SOUP
FRENCH ONION SOUP
& CRACKERBREAD

Quick Tomato Soup

To make this tomato soup you need a juice-maker. This is by far the easiest way of making fresh tomato soup and once you tried it you will be coming back for more. It can be made using different herbs, peppers and chili peppers, all to your own liking.

SERVES 2

10 tomatoes
1 onion
handful of basil
¼ of a vegetable stock cube
black pepper and salt to taste

INSTRUCTIONS:

1. Assemble juice-maker.
2. Juice tomatoes, onion and herbs.
3. Poor mixture into a saucepan.
4. Add stock cube and let it boil for a couple of minutes.

Pumpkin & Orange Soup

This recipe is very versatile and instead of orange one can add thai paste, chili flakes or anything else that suits your taste. The amount of ingredients is flexible depending on pumpkin size. So there might have to be a bit of tasting and tweaking before serving.

SERVES 4–6

1 medium de-seeded pumpkin cut into small square pieces
2 finely sliced onions
juice from 1 squeezed orange
water to cover pumpkin
2 vegetable stock cubes
100 ml cream
salt and pepper to taste

INSTRUCTIONS:

1. Add onions to a large saucepan (with a lid). Fry gently for 2 minutes.
2. Add pumpkin and water and boil until the pumpkin is soft.
3. Drain and save the water.
4. Blend the pumpkins and the onions to a smooth paste in a liquidiser.
5. Return the pumpkin mixture to the sauce pan. Add the stock cubes and the water for desired consistency.
6. Add orange juice and cream and stir.
7. Salt and pepper to taste and serve.

Broccoli & Stilton Soup

This is the perfect winter warmer. It is actually so filling it can be served as a main course. You do not have to use Stilton. Any hard blue cheese will do.

SERVES 2

500 g broccoli cut into pieces
50 g grated Stilton or other blue cheese
1 cube vegetable stock
250 ml of water
50 ml cream

INSTRUCTIONS:

1. Boil the broccoli in the water and the vegetable stock for 10–15 minutes.
2. Liquidise.
3. Return to saucepan and add grated Stilton and cream.
4. Stir well and serve.

Carrot & Onion Soup

This is a quick, tasty and healthy soup. To make this soup you need a liquidiser.

SERVES 2

1 chopped onion
2 thinly sliced carrots
25 g of butter or margarine
1 vegetable stock cube
450 ml water
125 ml milk
salt and pepper to taste

INSTRUCTIONS:

1. Melt the butter in a saucepan.
2. Add the onion and the thinly sliced carrots and fry gently for a couple of minutes.
3. Add the stock and let it simmer slowly for approximately 15 minutes.
4. Liquidise.
5. Return to the saucepan.
6. Add the milk and heat it. Serve.

French Onion Soup

In the original recipe the soup is topped with bread and Gruyère cheese and then cooked in the oven. In this recipe it's served with some gluten-free crackerbread instead (see recipe on the next page). But feel free to experiment.

SERVES 6

700 g finely sliced onions
2 minced cloves of garlic
50 g butter
2 tbsp olive oil
2 tsp sugar
1 litre of water
2 vegetable stock cubes
300 ml white wine
salt and pepper to taste

INSTRUCTIONS:

1. Melt the olive oil and the butter in a large saucepan.
2. Add onions, garlic and sugar and fry slowly for 30 minutes until brown and gooey.
3. Add water, stock cubes and wine. When it reaches boiling point, turn down to a low setting, and let it simmer for 1 hour.
4. Ready to eat!

Gluten-Free Crackerbread

This is a very healthy and tasty variation of a crackerbread that goes wonderfully with soup.

1 OVEN TRAY

65 g sunflower seeds
30 g sesame seeds
30 g linseeds
100 g gluten-free white flour
½ tsp salt
50 ml olive oil
200 ml boiling water

INSTRUCTIONS:

1. Preheat oven to 150° C.
2. Mix all the dry ingredients.
3. Add olive oil.
4. Add boiling water.
5. Put dough on a baking sheet. One easy way is to add another baking sheet on top and roll out the dough between the sheets forming one large flat crackerbread the size of the oven tray. This way the rolling pin doesn't get dirty. Just discard of the top baking sheet before baking the crackerbread in the oven.
6. Put the crackerbread in the oven and bake for 1 hour. Take out of the oven and let it cool down.
7. Break into manageable pieces. Can easily be made in bigger batches and stored in an airtight container.

salads

GREEK SALAD
SALATE TRICOLORE
STRAWBERRY & PARMESAN SALAD
LEMON & SAFFRON COUSCOUS
BEETROOT & GOAT CHEESE SALAD
WATERMELON & FETA SALAD
WALDORF SALAD

Greek Salad

There is nothing better than a Greek Salad on a warm day. It is important to pour some salt on top of the vegetables and let them sit and rest for a while. The juice from the tomatoes mixed with the olive oil serves as the dressing. Try and find the best ingredients for this dish- it really makes a big difference.

SERVE 4 AS A SIDE DISH

4 tomatoes cut into pieces
1 peeled and sliced cucumber
1 small finely sliced red onion
4 tbsp olive oil
1 ½ tsp dried oregano
200 g feta cheese crumbled
handful of Greek olives, pitted if you like

INSTRUCTIONS:

1. Put the vegetables in a large bowl and sprinkle them with salt. Let them rest for 20 minutes.
2. Add olive oil and the rest of the ingredients to the vegetables.
3. Serve.

Salate Tricolore

This easy salad is perfect as a starter but works well as a main course too. As in all recipes with few ingredients the quality of the ingredients is of utmost importance. Use the best tomatoes you can find and don't ever put them in your fridge. Tomatoes should be kept at room temperature or even better- be warm from the sun.

SERVES 2

4 tomatoes
1-2 avocados depending on size
one ball of mozzarella cheese
olive oil
red balsamic vinegar
salt and pepper to taste

INSTRUCTIONS:

1. Slice tomatoes, avocados and mozzarella.
2. Lay on two plates, resembling the Italian flag.
3. Poor olive oil and red balsamic vinegar over.
4. Salt and pepper to taste and enjoy.

Strawberry & Parmesan Salad

This might sound like a strange mix, but it tastes fantastic. The salty parmesan goes superbly with the sweet strawberries and the maple syrup in the dressing. Works well as a buffet salad as it looks nice when you serve it on a platter.

SERVES 6 AS A SIDE DISH

1 bag of baby spinach
2 handfuls of rocket salad
1 handful of pine nuts
1 box of cherry tomatoes cut in halves
10 sliced strawberries
parmesan to shave over the top

For the dressing:
1 part maple syrup
1 part white balsamic vinegar
2 parts olive oil

INSTRUCTIONS:

1. Put the baby spinach leaves on a big platter.
2. Add rocket, tomatoes, strawberries.
3. Sprinkle pine nuts over the salad.
4. Grate some parmesan over the salad.
5. Mix the dressing and pour over the salad.
6. Almost to pretty to eat!

Lemon & Saffron Couscous

Normal couscous is not gluten-free. To make this couscous you need to find a gluten-free couscous or use quinoa instead. The recipe makes a super-tasty dish which is great to serve as part of a buffet or on its own. Can be kept for at least 4 days in the fridge and tastes just as good hot or cold.

SERVES 6

300 g gluten-free couscous
500 ml water
½ tsp salt
2 cubes of vegetable stock
½ thinly sliced lemon
1 g of saffron
70 g raisins
100 g cashew nuts
1 finely diced red pepper
olive oil

INSTRUCTIONS:

1. Boil water, lemon, salt and stock cubes in a saucepan for 5 minutes.
2. Close the heat and add the couscous to the saucepan and let it sit and rest in the pan for 5 minutes with a lid.
3. Use a fork to separate the couscous and mix in some good olive oil.
4. Add raisins, cashew nuts and red pepper.
5. Stir and serve.

Beetroot & Goat Cheese Salad

This is a lovely filling salad. Perfect for anyone who loves beetroots. You can be flexible with the amount of ingredients. Some people want lots of goat cheese and some prefer more beetroots. Try it your way.

....

BUFFET

beetroots
salad for example baby spinach or rocket
goats cheese (preferably buy the one without the rind)

INSTRUCTIONS:

1. Boil beetroots until you can insert a skewer into the beetroot without to much force. This takes approximately 20 minutes.
2. Peel the beetroots and cut them into chunks small enough to fit in your mouth.
3. Cut the goat's cheese into small squares.
4. Mix beetroot, salad and goat cheese.
5. Serve with balsamic vinegar and olive oil and a piece of gluten-free bread.

Watermelon & Feta Salad

This is a very refreshing salad to eat when it is just too hot to eat anything else. You can be flexible with the amount.

BUFFET

watermelon cut into small chunks
feta cheese cut into small squares
pitted black olives
couple of handfuls of salad
for example iceberg lettuce cut finely

INSTRUCTIONS:

1. Mix ingredients to your liking.
2. Eat in the shade.

Waldorf Salad

A hot jacket potato is the ideal comfort food. This Waldorf Salad is a highly suitable accompaniment.

....

MAKES A BIG BOWL

4 diced Golden Delicious Apples
1 tbsp lemon juice
1 ½ tbsp sugar
½ tsp lemon juice (for the mayonnaise mix)
118 g chopped celery
118 g halved green grapes
118 g chopped walnuts
70 g raisins
100 g mayonnaise
150 ml cream
nutmeg to garnish

INSTRUCTIONS:

1. Put the diced apples in a big bowl and sprinkle with lemon juice.
2. Add celery, grapes, walnuts and raisins.
3. Combine mayonnaise with lemon juice.
4. Whip cream with sugar until fairly stiff.
5. Fold together cream and mayonnaise and mix with the fruits.
6. Sprinkle with nutmeg and chill for at least 1 hour before serving.

main courses

HOMEMADE PASTA	MANICOTTO
SPINACH RISOTTO	GLUTEN-FREE PIZZA
GREEK OMELETTE	PASTA CAPRESE
CHEDDAR QUICHE	BUBBLE & SQUEAK
VODKA PENNE	LEMON SPAGETTI
FENNEL GRATIN	POLPETTONE
CASHEW NUT CURRY	GREEK VEGGIE MOUSSAKA
ALMOND BALLS	INDIAN LENTIL DHAL
ITALIAN ALMOND BALLS	MACARONI & CHEESE
KORMA ALMOND BALLS	BUTTERNUT SQUASH CURRY
SPICY ALMOND BALLS	COURGETTE PASTA

Homemade Gluten-Free Pasta

This pasta is really easy to make so it is worth giving it a go. You do not have to use a pasta machine just make sure you roll out the dough thinly and use a knife to cut it into thin ribbons. In this picture it has been mixed with a handful of chopped parsley, some fried garlic, chili flakes and a drizzling of olive oil.

SERVES 4

100 g rice flour
100 g corn flour
3 tbsp potato flour
2 tsp xanthan gum
3 large eggs or 4 small
1,5 tbsp olive oil

polenta to roll the pasta in

INSTRUCTIONS:

1. Add all the ingredients into a kitchen machine. Blend for a minute until a big ball of dough is formed.
2. Wrap the ball of dough in clingfilm and leave in the fridge for at least 30 minutes.
3. Flour a surface with rice flour. Roll the dough into a thin layer, approximately 1 mm thick. Cut thin ribbons and put in a big dish and mix them with a handful of polenta. The polenta keeps the pasta ribbons from sticking together. Once you boil the pasta the polenta falls off.
4. Boil the pasta in a large saucepan with water and 1 tsp of salt for 30 seconds. Serve.

Spinach Risotto

This is a tasty risotto recipe. The spinach adds extra vitamins and irons.

....

SERVE 4

320 g Avorio rice
800-900 ml vegetable stock
1 chopped onion
2 handfuls of frozen chopped spinach
1 minced clove of garlic
1 glass of white wine
80 g grated parmesan cheese
2 tbsp cream (optional)

INSTRUCTIONS:

1. Fry onion and garlic in a bit of olive oil for 2 minutes.
2. Add the rice and coat it with the olive oil.
3. Add a glass of white wine.
4. When there is hardly any wine left start adding vegetable stock, one ladle at the time.
5. After 15 minutes add the spinach. Continue to add vegetable stock.
6. Cook for another 10 minutes. When the risotto is soft but still have a nice chew to it, it is ready.
7. Add parmesan cheese and cream if you like and stir it into the risotto. Serve.

Greek Omelette

This omelette is a great example on how you easy can transform an ordinary dish into something extraordinary with a few well chosen ingredients.

SERVES 4

3 diced tomatoes
200 g crumbled feta cheese
4 eggs
250 ml cream
½ tsp salt
pinch of black pepper
3 big handfuls of chopped rocket salad

INSTRUCTIONS:

1. Pre-heat oven to 225° C.
2. Put the diced tomatoes in a colander to drain off some of its excess juice.
3. Whisk together eggs, cream, salt and pepper.
4. Add tomatoes, rocket and feta cheese to a buttered oven dish.
5. Pour over the egg mixture.
6. Cook in oven for 30-40 minutes.
7. Serve with a green salad.

Cheddar Quiche

This is the best quiche there is! There is a Swedish cheese called Västerbotten that is ideal for this recipe, but if you can't get hold of it, an extra matured cheddar will work really well too.

SERVE 4–6

For the dough:
60 g sesame seeds
150 g gluten-free white flour
125 g butter
pinch of salt

The filling:
1 finely chopped leek
3 chopped onions
3 minced cloves of garlic
1 tsp salt
1 tsp sugar
1 tbsp dried thyme
80 g grated cheese
2 eggs
200 g cream

INSTRUCTIONS:

1. Pre-heat oven to 200° C.
2. Mix ingredients for the dough, preferably in a kitchen machine otherwise in a bowl with a knife.
3. Press the dough out into a pie oven dish. Prick with a fork and leave in the fridge while making the filling.
4. Fry leek, onions, garlic, thyme and sugar in a pan with olive oil. Don't let them catch any colour.
5. Mix together cream, eggs, salt and a sprinkling of pepper.
6. Bake the dough in the pie dish for 10 minutes. Take it out of the oven.
7. Add leek mixture, cheese and the cream mixture. Bake for 25 minutes. Serve.

Vodka Penne

Vodka Penne doesn't taste of vodka. It is made of a rich tomato sauce. Very quick and easy to make, yet so much flavour with every mouthful.

SERVES 2

150 g gluten-free penne pasta
½ chopped onion
1 minced clove of garlic
1 can (400g) crushed tomatoes
2 tbsp olive oil
1 tsp sugar
1 tsp dried basil
¼ cube of vegetable stock
2 tbsp cream
1 tbsp of vodka
salt and pepper to taste
parmesan for serving

INSTRUCTIONS:

1. Boil gluten-free penne in a large saucepan. Follow instructions on package
2. Gently fry onions and garlic in olive oil in a small saucepan for approximately 3 minutes.
3. Add can of tomatoes, stock, sugar and basil and let it all simmer slowly under a lid for 15-20 minutes.
4. Drain the penne when it is ready and return to saucepan.
5. Pour the vodka on the penne and stir.
6. Add cream to tomato sauce and stir.
7. Add tomato sauce to the pasta and mix well.
8. Serve with grated parmesan, salt and pepper.

Fennel Gratin

This is a lovely gratin that can be eaten on its own or as an accompaniment to another dish.

SERVE 4 AS A SIDE DISH

800 g fennel cut into thin wedges
2 diced tomatoes
125 g mozzarella cheese cut into small squares
40 g grated parmesan cheese
salt and pepper to taste

INSTRUCTIONS:

1. Pre-heat oven to 225° C.
2. Boil the fennel wedges for 2 minutes. Assemble fennel, tomatoes and mozzarella cheese in a buttered oven dish.
3. Sprinkle with parmesan cheese and salt and pepper.
4. Bake in oven for 20 minutes.
5. Serve as a side dish or with a green salad as a main course.

Cashew Nut Curry

This curry is so versatile and easy to make. You do not have to use the vegetables suggested. A frozen bag of wok-mix will work well too.

SERVE 2

1 dl cashew nuts
vegetables such as red onion, bamboo shoots, water chestnuts, green beans and baby corn works well but you can also use a ready mix of frozen vegetables to create a quick tasty meal
1 tbsp of curry powder
300 ml water
1 vegetable stock cube
100 ml cream

INSTRUCTIONS:

1. Fry vegetables and curry powder in olive oil and for 7 minutes.
2. Add the water and stock cube and let it simmer for 15 minutes without a lid.
3. Add the cashew nuts.
4. Add the cream. You can thicken the sauce slightly if you like, with your own preferred method (see page 5).
5. Serve with basmati rice and green salad.

Almond Balls

These almond balls are the perfect replacement for meatballs. They are so versatile and can be plunged into any sauce of your liking. You need a blender for this recipe. Remember to roll them into small balls because they grow when being boiled.

SERVE 4

75 g almonds blended into flour
80 g gluten-free breadcrumbs
60 g grated cheddar cheese
2 tbsp grated onion
1 tsp salt
good grinding of black pepper
3 eggs

To boil in:
1 litre of water
1 vegetable stock cube

INSTRUCTIONS:

1. Mix all the ingredients.
2. Form mixture into small balls.
3. Boil the small balls in the water with the added stock cube for 8 minutes.
4. Use a spoon sieve to separate the balls from the hot liquid.
5. Fry the balls in olive oil in a pan until golden colour. Eat as they are or add to a sauce of your choice.

Italian Almond Balls

This tomato sauce is very quick and easy to make. Add the almond balls when almost ready and serve with spagetti.

SERVE 2

150 g gluten-free spagetti
½ chopped onion
1 minced clove of garlic
1 can (400g) crushed tomatoes
2 tbsp olive oil
1 tsp sugar
1 tsp dried oregano
¼ cube of vegetable stock
salt and pepper to taste

INSTRUCTIONS:

1. Gently fry onions and garlic in olive oil in a small saucepan for approximately 3 minutes.
2. Add can of tomatoes, stock, sugar and oregano and let it all simmer slowly for 15-20 minutes.
3. When there is approximately 5 minutes left add almond balls to the sauce.
4. Serve with spagetti.

Korma Almond Balls

Korma sauce is a tasty creamy sauce full of Indian spices. It is easy and quick to make and goes perfectly with the vegetarian almond balls and some basmati rice.

SERVE 2

2 diced tomatoes
½ chopped onion
1 finely chopped garlic clove
¼ tsp chili flakes
1 tsp ground cinnamon
1 tsp ground cardamom
½ tsp ground cumin
200 ml cream

INSTRUCTIONS:

1. Fry onions for a few minutes. Do not let them catch any colour.
2. Add tomatoes and garlic and fry for a minute.
3. Add the spices and the cream and stir.
4. Add the almond balls and make sure they get heated thoroughly.
5. Serve with salad and basmati rice.

Spicy Almond Balls

This tangy pepper sauce works as a perfect accompaniment to the almond balls. If you like a thicker sauce it can be thickened using cornflour or potato flour (see page 5).

SERVES 2

1 finely sliced red pepper
1 finely sliced onion
¼ vegetable stock cube
300 ml water
¼ tsp chili flakes or to taste
1 tsp paprika powder
100 ml cream

INSTRUCTIONS:

1. Fry peppers and onion slices in a little bit of olive oil. Don't let it catch any colour.
2. Add water, stock cube and spices and let it simmer on a low heat for approximately 15-20 minutes.
3. Add cream and almond balls and simmer just to make them thoroughly warm.
4. Serve with a green salad and fried potatoes or rice.

Gluten–Free Manicotto

In this recipe the pancakes work as a sort of cannelloni, capturing all the delicious cheese and herbs. Best served with a plain green salad.

SERVES 4

For the pancakes:
300 ml water
150 g gluten-free white flour
4 eggs
pinch of salt and pepper
(makes 8 pancakes)

For the pancake filling:
500 g ricotta cheese
60 g grated parmesan
1 tsp dried basil
1 tsp dried oregano

For the topping:
600 ml of basil flavoured tomato sauce
100 g grated mozzarella

INSTRUCTIONS:

1. Pre-heat oven to 175° C.
2. Start by making the pancakes. Mix the flour and water well. Make sure there are no lumps. Add eggs and salt and pepper.
3. Fry an 1/8 of the mixture on one side in a pan in a little olive oil.
4. Put it with the cooked side up on a plate. Finish making all the pancakes.
5. Mix the ingredients for the filling and add an 1/8 of the filling to each of the pancakes
6. Fold pancakes into long cigars and put in a buttered oven dish. Make sure the fold is in under. Add the tomato sauce on top of the pancakes and cook in the oven for 30 minutes. Add the grated mozzarella and cook for 15 minutes. Serve with a salad.

Gluten-Free Pizza

This is a great recipe for gluten-free pizza. Served here with a classic topping of tomato sauce, mozzarella cheese and basil leaves. You can of course add your own favourite topping.

MAKES 1 BIG PIZZA OR 2 SMALL

30 g yeast (preferable fresh)
200 ml of lukewarm water
2 tbsp olive oil
1 tsp salt
300 g gluten-free white flour

INSTRUCTIONS:

1. Mix the yeast with the water.
2. Add olive oil, salt and gluten-free flour.
3. Mix thoroughly preferable in a kitchen machine but you can use your hands as well.
4. Let it rise to double its size.
5. Pre-heat the oven to 225° C.
6. Flatten the dough into a pizza shape on a non-stick baking sheet placed on an oven tray.
7. Cook it in the oven for 7 minutes.
8. Add topping and cook for an additional 10-15 minutes until ready.

Pasta Caprese

This is so easy to make, yet so tasty. Make sure you use excellent tomatoes and you can't go wrong. You can use any type of short pasta for this recipe.

SERVE 2

140 g gluten-free pasta
3 diced tomatoes
1 finely chopped garlic
200 g diced mozzarella
big handful of chopped fresh basil leaves
olive oil
red balsamic vinegar
salt and pepper to taste

INSTRUCTIONS:

1. Boil pasta in a large saucepan and drain when ready.
2. Transfer pasta back to saucepan and add tomatoes, mozzarella, garlic and basil.
3. Stir well and add olive oil, red balsamic vinegar and salt and pepper.
4. Serve and enjoy.

Bubble & Squeak

This is a very tasty winter dish for anyone who likes cabbage. In England this dish is called Bubble and Squeak and in Ireland it is called Colcannon.

....

SERVE 4

3 big potatoes cut into small squares
50 g butter
1 tbsp olive oil
2 finely sliced onions
1 small savoy cabbage (or a half if big) cut into small pieces
salt and pepper to taste

INSTRUCTIONS:

1. Pre-heat oven to 200° C.
2. Boil the potatoes for approximately 7 minutes. Don't allow them to get mushy.
3. Fry the onions in olive oil for 5 minutes on a moderate heat.
4. Fry the savoy cabbage in olive oil until it wilts.
5. Add potatoes, cabbage and onions to a buttered oven dish and mix thoroughly
6. Sprinkle with salt and pepper and dot small pieces of the butter over the dish.
7. Bake in the oven for approximately 20 minutes. Serve!

Lemon Pasta

This is a tasty pasta with lemon and fresh herbs. It is also very quick to make. The sauce is made whilst you boil the pasta, which means it does not need to take more than 10 minutes.

SERVE 2

140 g gluten- free spaghetti
zest from 1 lemon
1 handful of fresh coriander leaves
1 handful of fresh flat leaf parsley
1 handful of mint leaves
1 glass of white wine
100 ml cream
parmesan for grating
salt and pepper to taste

INSTRUCTIONS:

1. Boil pasta in a large saucepan. Follow instructions on the package.
2. Fry lemon zest for 1 minute in a little bit of olive oil. Chop all the herbs finely.
3. Add white wine and let it simmer until the wine is reduced to approximately half the amount.
4. Add cream and herbs.
5. Add a handful of grated parmesan cheese and stir.
6. Drain the spaghetti when it is ready and add it to the frying pan. Make sure to mix it well with the sauce.
7. Serve. Add additional grated parmesan and season with salt and pepper.

Polpettone di verdure

This vegetable loaf will make you dream about Italy. It is a ligurian dish that is naturally gluten-free, vegetarian and delicious.

SERVE 4–6

1 kilo potatoes
500 g courgette
1 can of cannellini beans
2 tbsp olive oil
100 g grated parmesan
2 minced cloves of garlic
1 bunch of parsley
4 eggs
approximately 20 fresh leaves of basil
salt and pepper to taste

INSTRUCTIONS:

1. Pre-heat the oven to 200° C.
2. Peel and dice the potatoes into cm large pieces.
3. Boil the diced potatoes in lightly salted water for 7 minutes. When finished let it drain.
4. Cut courgette in half and remove the core. Cut the remaining into pieces.
5. Boil courgette for 10 minutes, then drain.
6. Add the beans, courgette, parmesan, garlic, herbs, olive oil and eggs in a kitchen machine and mix well.
7. Fold the potatoes in the courgette mixture and pour into an oven dish.
8. Cook for 35 minutes.
9. Let it cool. Cut into squares and serve with rocket salad and a drizzling of olive oil.

Greek Veggie Moussaka

This is a wonderful vegetarian dish. By oven roasting the vegetables first it becomes so much more flavoursome.

SERVE 4

1 large aubergine cut into 5 mm slices
2 thickly sliced courgettes
2 onions cut into wedges
2 de-seeded and chopped red peppers
2 minced garlic cloves
5 tbsp olive oil
1 tbsp dried thyme
2 eggs whisked
300 ml Greek yoghurt
1 can (400 g) chopped tomatoes
55 g of feta cheese crumbled
salt and pepper to taste

INSTRUCTIONS:

1. Pre-heat the oven to 220° C.
2. Put aubergine in a colander with salt on top and leave for 20 minutes. Dry them off.
3. Add aubergine slices, onions, garlic, courgettes and red peppers in a large oven dish and sprinkle with the olive oil. Season with thyme and salt and pepper.
4. Bake the in oven for 30 minutes. When the vegetables are ready take them out of the oven and reduce the oven to 175° C.
5. Pour half the vegetables in an oven dish.
6. Cover with crushed tomatoes and add the rest of the vegetables on top.
7. Mix eggs, yoghurt, salt and pepper and pour over the vegetables. Sprinkle with feta.
8. Bake in the oven for 45 minutes. Enjoy!

Indian Lentil Dhal

This lentil dhal with its Indian spices is very nourishing. If you are lucky enough to find a gluten-free naan bread then it would be the perfect match. A gluten-free baguette works as a stand-in.

SERVE 4

1 chopped onion
2 minced garlic cloves
1 tsp cumin
2 tsp coriander
250 g red lentils
250 ml water
1 vegetable stock cube
1 can of coconut milk
2 tomatoes
1 bag of baby spinach
1 big handful of chopped coriander leaves

INSTRUCTIONS:

1. Fry onion and garlic with the spices in olive oil on a gentle heat in a large saucepan
2. Add lentils, water, stock cube and the coconut milk and let it simmer without a lid for 10 minutes.
3. Add chopped tomatoes and baby spinach to the saucepan and simmer for another 5 minutes.
4. Add salt and pepper to taste and sprinkle over the chopped coriander leaves.
5. Serve with some gluten-free bread or just a green salad.

Macaroni & Cheese

Macaroni cheese is a favourite with children and adults alike. There are many different versions. This one is gluten-free and vegetarian.

SERVE 2–3

150 g gluten-free macaroni
1 finely chopped onion
1 small head of cauliflower cut into chunks
300 ml milk
1 knob of butter
1 handful of grated cheddar cheese
1 handful of grated parmesan
1 pinch of cayenne pepper
1 tbsp potato flour
half a small cup of water
salt and pepper to taste

INSTRUCTIONS:

1. Pre-heat oven to 225° C.
2. Boil the macaroni. Follow instructions on the package. Add cauliflower to the macaroni when approximately 7 minutes of the boiling time remains.
3. Fry the chopped onion for approximately 3 minutes, take care not to let it colour.
4. In a large saucepan add the milk, butter, and a pinch of cayenne pepper. Mix potato flour with a little bit of water. When the milk reaches boiling point, slowly add the potato flour mixture a little at a time and stir vigorously, until the sauce gets the desired thickness. Add parmesan/salt/pepper and stir.
5. Add macaroni/cauliflower/onions to the white sauce. Put in an ovendish. Sprinkle with parmesan. Bake for 25 minutes.

Butternut Squash Curry

This is a tasty curry using butternut squash, spinach and feta cheese.

SERVE 2

1 butternut squash, peeled, de seeded and cut into small squares
1-2 diced tomatoes
1 onion finely chopped
1 tsp ground cumin
1 tsp ground coriander
200 g spinach
100 g feta cheese cut into little pieces
¼ tsp chili flakes or to taste

INSTRUCTIONS:

1. Pre-heat oven to 225° C.
2. Cook butternut squash squares in olive oil for 30 minutes in the oven.
3. Fry onion and the spices in a frying pan.
4. Add the spinach and fry for 2 minutes.
5. Add all the ingredients to the cooked butternut squash and mix well.
6. Ready to serve.

Courgette Pasta

This is a quick and tasty pasta recipe. Any type of short gluten-free pasta would do.

SERVE 2

140 g gluten-free fusilli
2 courgettes, cut in half and finely sliced
1 finely sliced onion
1 minced garlic clove
1 tsp dried basil
1 tsp dried thyme
olive oil
parmesan to serve

INSTRUCTIONS:

1. Boil pasta. Follow instructions on the package.
2. Fry the onions and garlic slowly in a frying pan, take care not to let them colour.
3. Fry the courgette slices in olive oil in the frying pan.
4. Add onions and herbs with the courgettes.
5. Drain pasta and add to the vegetables. Mix thoroughly.
6. Salt/pepper and sprinkle with parmesan.
7. Serve.

desserts

CHOCOLATE ICE CREAM
ETON MESS
SPANISH LEMON CAKE
STICKY CHOCOLATE CAKE
MERINGUE SWISH
APPLE CRUMBLE
GLUTEN-FREE WAFFLES
BLUEBERRY CHEESECAKE

Chocolate Ice Cream

This is a very easy way of making genuine tasting gelato- Italian ice cream. Of course you can add any fruit or flavour. In that case just ignore the cocoa powder.

....

MAKES 1,5 LITRES OF ICECREAM

500 ml cream
1 tin of condensed milk
3 tbsp cocoa powder
(use a good dark powder)
2 tsp vanilla powder

INSTRUCTIONS:

1. Add all ingredients to a bowl.
2. Whisk until it reaches soft peaks.
3. Pour into a freezing container.
4. Freeze for approximately 3-4 hours.
5. Ready to eat.

Eton Mess

This is a traditional English dessert. Very quick to make and very tasty. In this version raspberries are used but you can also use strawberries.

SERVE 6

1 bag of meringues
1 small bag frozen raspberries that has been de-frosted
300 ml cream
1 tsp vanilla powder
1 handful of fresh raspberries to decorate (optional)

INSTRUCTIONS:

1. Whip the cream with the vanilla powder until it reaches soft peaks.
2. Layer the dessert e.g. cream, meringues, raspberries and so on, in one big bowl or individual glasses.
3. Top with the fresh raspberries.
4. Serve.

Spanish Lemon Cake

This is a naturally gluten-free cake from Northern Spain, using ground almonds as flour. The lemons add a fresh flavour to the cake.

MAKES 1 CAKE

300 g finely ground almonds
4 eggs
250 g sugar
juice and zest of 1 lemon
1 tsp cinnamon

For lemon syrup:
juice and zest of 1 lemon
25 g sugar
icing sugar

INSTRUCTIONS:

1. Pre-heat oven to 160° C.
2. Blend the almonds until finely ground.
3. Whisk egg yolks, sugar, lemon zest and juice in a bowl until pale and fluffy.
4. Add the cinnamon and the ground almonds to the egg mixture.
5. Whisk egg whites until it form stiff peaks.
6. Fold the egg whites into the mixture.
7. Bake in the oven for 45 minutes.
8. Take the cake out and let it cool.
9. In the meantime make the syrup by putting the icing sugar and the zest and juice in a small saucepan and heat gently.
10. Pour over the cake and serve with whipped cream or as it is.

Sticky Chocolate Cake

This is the ultimate sticky runny chocolate cake. Serve it with whipped cream or a scoop of vanilla ice cream.

MAKES 1 CAKE

3 eggs
300 g sugar
100 g melted butter
75 g gluten-free white flour
1 ½ tsp vanilla powder
4 tbsp cocoa powder (use a dark variety)

INSTRUCTIONS:

1. Pre-heat oven to 175° C.
2. Melt the butter on a low heat.
3. Whisk eggs and sugar until light and fluffy.
4. Add gluten-free white flour, vanilla powder and cocoa powder to the egg mixture. Mix well.
5. Add the melted butter and mix.
6. Pour into a loose-bottomed cake tin.
7. Bake in oven for 20 minutes.
8. Let the cake rest for 30 minutes under a cloth, before serving with whipped cream or ice cream.

Meringue Swish

This is a popular dessert in Sweden. It needs to be assembled just before eating otherwise it will melt.

SERVE 6

1 bag of meringues
300 ml cream
1 tsp vanilla powder
half a litre of vanilla ice cream
3 chopped bananas

For the chocolate sauce:

1 part chocolate powder
(use a good dark powder)
1 part sugar
1 part water
large pinch of salt

INSTRUCTIONS:

1. Whip the cream with the vanilla powder until it reaches soft peaks.
2. Put the ingredients in a few layers e.g. ice cream, cream, bananas, meringue and so on.
3. Mix all ingredients for the chocolate sauce in a small saucepan. Heat it and let it simmer slowly for 3 minutes.
4. Serve meringue swish in bowls and pour chocolate sauce on top.
5. Eat and enjoy.

Apple Crumble

This apple crumble is a real treat. Serve it with a scoop of vanilla ice cream or whipped cream.

....

SERVE 6

6 apples (or approximately 800 g)
150 g butter
120 g gluten-free oats
200 g white sugar
50 ml white syrup
75 g gluten-free white flour
½ tsp baking powder
2 tbsp milk

INSTRUCTIONS:

1. Pre-heat the oven to 175° C.
2. Melt butter in a saucepan. Take off the heat.
3. Add all ingredients (except for the apples) to the butter.
4. Peel, cord and finely slice the apples.
5. Put the apple slices in a buttered oven dish.
6. Add the mixture on top of the apples.
7. Bake in the oven for approximately 30 minutes.

Gluten-Free Waffles

For this recipe you will need a waffle iron. It will probably be worth the investment because once you tasted those crispy tasty waffles- you will want to eat them again and again.

MAKES 5 WAFFLES

2 eggs
250 ml milk
125 g gluten-free white flour
2 tbsp melted butter
1 tsp baking powder
(make sure it is gluten-free)

INSTRUCTIONS:

1. Mix the gluten-free flour with the baking powder.
2. Separate the egg yolks from the whites in two different bowls.
3. Whisk the egg yolks with the milk.
4. Whisk the egg whites until hard.
5. Add flour mixture to the milk mixture.
6. Add the butter to milk mixture.
7. Fold in the egg whites carefully.
8. Heat the waffle iron.
9. Brush the iron with melted butter and add a ladle of mixture.
10. Cook and enjoy with whipped cream and strawberry jam.

Blueberry Cheesecake

This cheesecake does not need an oven. For this recipe you need to find a packet of gluten-free digestives.

....

MAKES 1 CAKE

For the base:
200 g gluten-free digestives
100 g melted butter

For the filling:
500 g mascarpone cheese
500 ml crème fraiche
3 tbsp icing sugar
zest from 2 lemons

For the topping:
350 g blueberries, de-frosted
100 ml fresh lemon juice
125 g sugar

INSTRUCTIONS:

1. Boil the ingredients for the topping slowly for 15 minutes. Take off heat and cool slightly.
2. Mix digestives and melted butter in a kitchen machine.
3. Press mixture into a loose-bottomed cake tin.
4. Mix the ingredients for the filling and add to the top of the base.
5. Pour the topping over the cake and leave to set in the fridge for at least 3 hours.

Author & Photographer: Ann Brooke-Webb

Layout & Publishing: Ann Brooke-Webb

Printed by CreateSpace. An Amazon.com Company

Available from Amazon.com and other retail outlets.

Available on Kindle and other devises.

Printed in Great Britain
by Amazon